# JOURNEY TO MY
# FUTURE**NOW**

CHRIS MUSGROVE

An incredible true story

of discovering vision, gifting & purpose.

# JOURNEY TO MY FUTURENOW!
## FutureNow – The Story

Copyright © 2021 Chris Musgrove

Published by Book Ripple Publishing
www.BookRipple.com

All scriptures are taken from the New King James Version unless otherwise noted. Scripture taken from the New King James Version. Copyright © 1979, 1980, 1982 by Thomas Nelson, Inc. Used by permission. All rights reserved. / Holy Bible, New International Version®, NIV® Copyright ©1973, 1978, 1984, 2011 by Biblica, Inc.® Used by permission. All rights reserved worldwide. / GOD'S WORD is a copyrighted work of God's Word to the Nations. Quotations are used by permission. Copyright 1995 by God's Word to the Nations. All rights reserved. / Scripture taken from The Message. Copyright © 1993, 1994, 1995, 1996, 2000, 2001, 2002. Used by permission of NavPress Publishing Group. / Scripture quotations are from the ESV® Bible (The Holy Bible, English Standard Version®), copyright © 2001 by Crossway Bibles, a publishing ministry of Good News Publishers. Used by permission. All rights reserved. / Scripture quotations from the COMMON ENGLISH BIBLE. © Copyright 2011 COMMON ENGLISH BIBLE. All rights reserved. Used by permission. (www.CommonEnglishBible.com). / Scripture taken from the NEW AMERICAN STANDARD BIBLE®, Copyright © 1960, 1962, 1963, 1968, 1971, 1972, 1973, 1975, 1977, 1995 by The Lockman Foundation. Used by permission.

ISBN: 978-1-951797-31-7
Printed in the United States of America

To reach the author, go to:
www.futurenow.us
www.chrismusgroveministries.com

# WHAT OTHERS ARE SAYING

"I want to recommend to you the ministry and life of Chris Musgrove and his book, *Journey to My FutureNow*. I have served as a pastor to Chris and walked with him for many years. He is a gifted man of God with a pure heart that not only hears the voice of God but quickly obeys. In addition to his heart of obedience, he walks in great boldness and is a man of great humility. In this book, you will be encouraged and motivated to give your best to the Lord, and as you do, you will see God's blessing on your obedience."

> — *L. A. Joiner*
> *Pastor and Apostolic Leader, Saint*
> *Augustine, FL*

---

"Chris Musgrove paints an exciting journey of learning to surrender solely to the Lord. From taking life-altering risks to encountering the sovereignty of God amongst a difficult atmosphere, Chris shows us that we can all be used by the Lord if we lay down our own desires

3

and follow His divine plan. From cover to cover, you will be encouraged, inspired, but most importantly, you will be challenged to live a life that is undeniably sold out to Christ and ready to preach His glorious Gospel. To think he was a part of the youth group my husband and I led years ago and that we had just a small part in such a big picture, you just never know who you will be able to reach for Christ and how your fruit will truly remain. If you are on the fence of following God's purpose for your life, allow Chris's story to compel you to follow the voice of the Holy Spirit and step out of the boat with outrageous boldness and faith!"

> – *Jeri Hill*
> *Evangelist and President of Steve Hill Ministries, Gulf Shores, AL*

---

"Chris Musgrove served as my youth pastor for 17 years. He was the most enthusiastic, passionate, faithful, and sometimes craziest, person I ever worked with in the ministry. In his new book, *Journey to My FutureNow*, Chris reveals how God rescued him from a life of sin and gave him a purpose and a vision to reach young people with the gospel of Jesus Christ.

Filled with inspiration, vision, and passion, this book will motivate you to discover God's will for your life and to do it. Told simply and succinctly through stories and episodes of his own life, *Journey to My FutureNow* paints a picture of how you can find your FutureNow and be all that God called you to be."

> *— Frank C. Davis*
> *Pastor, Author, and Mayor*
> *Live Oak, FL*

---

"Truly Inspiring! When I read *Journey to My FutureNow*, I was instantly stirred to fulfill things that had been in my heart for a long time. Chris Musgrove's story is not only miraculous, but it is also a roadmap to seeing your dreams come true. Get ready to have your heart stirred to do something significant for your generation! This book will be fuel to your fire!"

> *— Spencer & Cyndy Nordyke*
> *Nordyke Ministries, Dallas, TX*

---

"Chris Musgrove is a man on a mission from God. His life journey is one that changes lives — internally, externally and eternally. I read his story from start to finish in one sitting. I am honored to endorse it."

> – *Mick Hubert*
> *Voice of the Florida Gators,*
> *Gainesville, FL*

---

"It is written in Revelation 12:11, 'We overcome by the Blood of the Lamb and the Word of our testimony.' That is the story of Chris Musgrove. What an encouraging, inspiring, motivating, short, and to-the-point testimony for anyone who needs to re-fuel and re-fire their lives to finish strong."

> – *Joe McGee*
> *Minister, Author, and National*
> *Conference Speaker, Tulsa, OK*

---

"When Chris Musgrove entered my ninth-grade English class, I saw a young man with limitless potential and a contagious spark for life. Chris was a wonderful communicator and leader, but he was not ready to accept God's 'vision' or purpose for his life. As an educator, I always believed that, in addition to teaching the subject matter, I was to be an encourager for these young people. These students were only at the beginning stages of their lives, and they needed help in navigating these formative years of their lives while they tried to find their place in this world. In his book, *Journey to My FutureNow,* Chris details his personal journey to finding God's perfect will and vision for his life. Chris reveals how he surrendered his life to Christ and how he has a passion to help today's young people know that Jesus Christ is all they need to survive and to have meaning in this life. The book is an inspiring and encouraging revelation of how faith and commitment to God's will and God's timing can change lives, provide hope for the hopeless, and ultimately lead to eternal life through Jesus Christ. I highly recommend *Journey to My FutureNow.* This book is a powerful testimony of how God will lead and direct our paths in life if we open our hearts to His Word and His Truth! Thank you, Chris, for the difference you are making in young people's lives. God Bless you and your ministry at FutureNow."

> — *Shirley Allbritton*
> *(Chris's ninth-grade English Teacher),*
> *Suwannee High School, Live Oak, FL*

---

"Most people grow up wanting to be 'the hero' in their story. Chris Musgrove decided to follow Jesus and become a 'hero maker.' He has invested his life in leading the next generation into a relationship with Jesus. Those 'heroes' now dot the globe and are world changers. You will love this story, and it will inspire you to be a 'hero maker' in your life as well."

> – *John Nuzzo*
> *Victory Family Church, Pastor,*
> *Cranberry Township, PA*

"As director for the Fellowship of Christian Athletes in Georgia for 25 years, I have known Chris for some time. We have partnered with FutureNow on many occasions and have seen God do some great things in our schools. I have always been impressed that it is never about Chris or FutureNow but Christ, and how they can partner with other ministries and churches to see lives changed for His glory. Chris is a gifted leader and communicator who surrounds himself with other people who are gifted and passionate about the ministry God has called them to. I enjoyed reading his story of how God took an underachieving, troubled young man like himself and used him, and is still using him for his Kingdom purposes. It is a book that will encourage others to examine their own gifts and talents and begin to see how God wants to use them for His work on this earth."

> – *Dicky Clark*
> *Georgia State Director, Fellowship of Christian Athletes, Athens, GA*

---

"Chris Musgrove has been a personal friend of mine and a ministry colleague for many years. The passion, diligence, and determined pursuit he has exhibited in apprehending his God-given assignment has been an inspiration and an example not only to me, but to many others as well. I'm so thankful that Chris has taken the time to articulate and to pen his journey. I know it will be a source of encouragement to you and to all of those who, like Chris, are determined to apprehend that for which Christ has apprehended them. Take your time, read every word, because hidden within the pages of *Journey to My FutureNow*, you'll observe how Chris navigated the various seasons of his life and ministry, taking his divine cues, being in the right place at the right time – following the inward witness of the Spirit – all of these valuable keys that will give you personal insight and wisdom in both navigating and fulfilling your own destiny."

> – *Rev. Marty Blackwelder*
> *Blackwelder Ministries, Atlanta, GA*

———————————————

"FutureNow – its inception, work, and vision – this is what we call a 'God thing'! I am so glad to see the inspiration and illumination put into words in order to tell the story of the Musgroves and this special ministry. Now others can know why FutureNow and its pioneering family are so near and dear to my heart!"

> – *Dr. Bill Truby*
> *Principal, School Superintendent, and*
> *University Professor, Ocala, FL*

———————————————

"Wow, I can't express how excited I am having just read Chris Musgrove's book, *Journey to my FutureNow*. I first met Chris when we were both youth pastors in Florida. He brought a team of youth from his church who were on a mission to win other youth to Christ through singing, drama, skits, and preaching. It inspired us to do the same with our youth group, and we took them on a mission's trip to Trinidad. The youth were so amazed that God would use them to win souls that one girl started her own ministry at age 16 when we got back home. She is a full-time children's pastor and director of evangelism at her church today, along with her husband and their four kids, some 28 years later. I was so delighted to read about the journey that the Lord has taken Chris and his family on to come to the place where they are today, in full-time outreach ministry along with an awesome team, winning high school students to the Lord throughout South Georgia and North Florida. They actually go into the schools to do special assemblies, demonstrating life course correction through – you guessed it – music, drama, and motivational speaking. Then a Christian Bible club invites them to conduct a full evangelistic outreach that night, with hundreds and even thousands returning to receive Christ as savior or rededicate their lives back to the Lord. I can't think of a more vital ministry than to seal the deal of eternal life with young high school students, the future of America and the world. Chris's story is so engaging and full of spiritual wisdom, as he testifies of all of the great direction he received from the Lord, along with all of the many miracles that have transpired to bring them to the high level of effectiveness that they have reached. This will be a great read and an encouragement to every youth pastor and every lead pastor who wants to impact their community for God's kingdom. The methods are reproducible, and the training distinctive. I am sure you will thoroughly enjoy reading about how FutureNow was fully developed, and I pray that you will be inspired to partner with such a dynamic and successful ministry as they forge ahead to greater and greater success."

— *Dr. Douglas Wingate*
*President and Founder of Life Christian*
*University, Tampa, FL*

---

"The successful synopsis of any journey is not just how well you navigate through it, but how well you documented the details and paid attention to the empowerment of its purpose and pursuits. This book is a diagnostic revelation from beginning to end on all of the above. It underlines the importance of God-dot connections (a biography of God's kingdom fulfillments) and the type of faith in relationships and opportunities to make a vision in life full of God's work. This book explains, reveals, and explodes in a detailed fashion what one life can do with fulfillment when its fullness of pursuits is measured by God and His dot-connections. You will love this book. It will inspire you to step out into the unknown. Take advantage of every appreciated connection. And step out with a fulfilled, knowing already insight. Now, let your own journey be written. This book will inspire and encourage you to do so. BOOM!!!"

> – *Steve Munds*
> *Go Ministries, Shreveport, LA*

———————

"There is no success without succession! Jesus said, 'Go and make disciples' in Matthew 28. For 30 years I have served with Chris and Terri Musgrove. Watching their children grow up and now serving in ministry proves to me that they are making disciples at home! I am grateful that the gospel is being carried now by our children! Success!"

> – *Steve Mchargue*
> *North Florida Fellowship of Christian Athletes Staff, Madison, FL*

———————

"Whenever God wants to do something special, He calls a person and anoints them in a special way for that task. The person never feels qualified to do God's work, but God takes them through a supernatural process to prepare them. That is exactly what happened with Chris Musgrove! His testimony will inspire you to surrender to the Lord fully. And the results of his obedience will encourage you to say 'Yes' to the Holy Spirit. I am so glad Chris said 'Yes!' His bold steps of surrender resulted in many, many young people finding Jesus Christ personally."

> – *J. Lee Grady*
> *Author and Director of the Mordecai*
> *Project, LaGrange, GA*

---

"Reading *Journey to My FutureNow* is like journeying with a friend. I trust you will be inspired and challenged by Chris's book. He is an amazing friend of many years and a great example to the young men and women of our generation. He and Terri first came to Scotland in the early nineties, and their outreach to young people had a great impact on our church and community. We went from eight to eighty in our youth after their visit. I encourage you to read this book!"

> – *Pastor Bernie Mclaughlin*
> *Kilwining, Scotland UK*

---

"A Passion for our young people. The name Chris Musgrove and the FutureNow program come immediately to mind – and heart. His book explores the how to's, successes, and challenges of launching a nationwide ministry to our youth, a ministry that is making a difference. Chris keeps it real while empowering the readers with the sense that all of us have a part to play in changing lives for God's kingdom."

> – *Pastor Carol Kearns*
> *Lighthouse Word Church, Chiefland, FL*

---

"I consider it a great honor to recommend *Journey to My FutureNow*. It is an inspiring story of a man whose vision was to influence as many young people as possible in his lifetime. Our relationship began over 36 years ago when Chris became a student at Rhema Bible Training College in 1983 and graduated in 1985. Through the years, I've watched his ministry grow and have a positive impact on the Body of

Christ. He challenges people to have a deeper revelation of the Word and a more intimate relationship with God. As you read the pages of this book, you will be inspired to seek God for your future. I encourage you to raise your expectation and realize you have a purpose. This book will help you discover your destiny with God."

> *– Kenneth W. Hagin*
> *President, Kenneth Hagin Ministries &*
> *Rhema Bible Training College Pastor,*
> *Rhema Bible Church, Tulsa, OK*

---

"You are privileged to have a copy of this book in your hands. This tool will propel you towards your desires in life. The pages in this book will inspire you, guide you, and encourage you. You will see how God leads each of us step by step to our destiny – as we allow Him to lead us there. Enjoy this great work of personal transformation and victory and allow it to lead you to works of greatness."

> *– Pastor Bill Krause*
> *Family Community Church, North*
> *Highlands, CA*

---

"When I was asked to write an endorsement for this book, I thought about what words I could write that would be worthy of the respect I have for Chris and his family's complete and total commitment to God's call and heart for ministry to the youth. What can be more important in this day and age than to reach our youth? We must realize that they are God's future in this world! There's no doubt that many of the challenges we are faced with in today's society could have been by-passed by a more Christian, Bible-based upbringing in many of our homes and lives. Thank God we have a 'Chris Musgrove' in such a time as this – to bring the very life, principles, and Godly direction to our upcoming generations. With a man of God like Chris, we can look to the future with great hope and peace, that all will be well in the future House of God! As a pastor, I know the importance of the call and anointing God places on certain ones for this most necessary ministry. Without a doubt, I can vouch for (and I give thanks to God) that Chris has that special call. I am extremely grateful for the way he has helped our local church, too, whenever we needed his assistance. In my own personal life, he is a dear friend and I recognize with the utmost certainty he is a special man of God, with a special and unique call of God on His life. It's my honor to write an endorsement for this book, having great confidence that it will be a tremendous blessing to you!"

> – *Pastor Geri Moore*
> *Words of Life Fellowship Church, North*
> *Miami Beach, FL*

---

"'Increase our faith!' was the cry of the Apostles to the Lord (Luke 17:5). In his book, *Journey to My FutureNow*, Chris Musgrove shares his journey of increasing faith as God birthed a consuming passion for students in his soul. He shares stories of the Lord's supernatural provision, prophetic direction, and paints a vivid picture of the divine process of preparation that is essential for any who want to walk in the fullness of God's calling. The book will encourage you and increase your faith. I wholeheartedly endorse the ministry and message of Chris and FutureNow."

> – *Pastor Ken Cline*
> *New Life Christian Fellowship,*
> *Saginaw, MI*

---

"Chris Musgrove has written a book about youth ministry. But it is about way more than that. It's a book about the power of a heavenly vision. This book will stir your heart and cause you to see that an ordinary person can accomplish great things when he courageously follows God's plan for his life. I was blessed by this book. You will be, too."

— *Pastor Edwin Anderson*
*Impact Family Church, High Springs, FL*

"Chris's inspiring story relays the power of purpose and trusting God to bring it to pass in your life. I enjoyed seeing his passion for youth during his visit to Liverpool. His zeal is infectious and his ability to press through in spite of obstacles challenges the reader to press into all God has predestined for your life."

— *Pastor Di Stacey*
*Grace Family Church, Liverpool England*

"The story of Chris Musgrove and FutureNow will inspire you towards small steps of obedience and the impact that a committed life to Christ will make. Each and every detail through this book ignites a passion to discover the vision of

God for your life and the role He would have you play in reaching those around you. God has truly used Chris and FutureNow to reach a generation at such a pivotal time in their lives. This book will show you that simple acts of obedience lead to great rewards for the Kingdom of God."

— *Pastor Mark Brady*
*Anchor Faith Church, Valdosta, GA*

---

"As I read this book, I could literally hear Chris's voice... on one hand talking himself into moving forward, on the other hand overly excited about the journey God has him on. *Journey to My FutureNow* will bless you, push you, excite you, and motivate you to get involved."

— *Congressman Markwayne Mullin*
*Westville, Oklahoma*

# DEDICATION

I dedicate this book to my parents, Aulden and Frances Musgrove, who raised me and all five of my siblings in the fear and admonition of the Lord. They have both gone home to be with our Lord, but they left a great legacy of faith and trust in God.

I also want to dedicate this book to my wonderful wife Terri and my four children: Kasey, Christian, Victoria, and Isaac. Of all my accomplishments, I would have to place being a husband to Terri and a father to my four awesome children at the top! They have faithfully served with me as youth pastors, pastors, and evangelists.

Everything that I have ever done and accomplished in ministry has been a result of my wonderful family's support and willingness to go and give of themselves in order to live out the Gospel. Much of this story is theirs as well as mine. I love them dearly!

I also want to dedicate this book to all the many people who served as team members, interns, volunteers, prayer partners, and supporters. You have made this journey possible!

Lastly, I dedicate this book to my God and King, the Lord Jesus Christ, and the precious Holy Spirit, without whom there would be no transformed Chris Musgrove! To God be the glory!!!!!!

## Acknowledgements

When I began this project, I had no idea the amount of work required to publish a book. This has been a three-year process and required the help of many wonderful and gifted people.

I first want to thank my wife Terri for her continual support and advice in helping me complete this book.

My staff, family, and friends who put up with me in this process.

Dr. Bill Truby, who has been an asset to me in editing and re-editing, and re-editing! Thank you for not letting me quit or growing tired of my edit changes. Bill, you have become a trusted friend and brother! I also want to thank his wonderful wife, Sherry, for allowing him to be the blessing he is to our ministry!

Sue Keith, my long-time grant writer who also assisted in editing and research.

Lauren Lewis, my sister, who took my story to another level! Thank you for those three days in St. Augustine, FL and for all the food and coffee as we took the book from a good story to a great story! Your knowing me and how I function allowed you to pull things out of me as we wrote and rewrote until we got it right. Your ability to hear from the Spirit of God and articulate what I was thinking was powerful! You, my sister have a gift and I thank you for using it for this book! I love you!

Jason Taylor, my videographer and photographer who came up with the book cover concept, along with his wonderful wife, Savannah.

Brian Mast, my publisher who I have known for many years. I am so thankful that we finally got to do a book together! I thank God for the connection we made many years ago. Thank you for your patience with me in getting this book together!

I want to thank all the wonderful Christian leaders who took the time to read my manuscript and to share their helpful comments and endorsements for the book and our ministry. You will never know how much you blessed me and our ministry by the wonderful things you said! God bless you all!

Lastly, I want to thank all our wonderful partners that give time and time again and pray for us daily so that we are able to fulfill the call God has placed on our lives! We thank God for you and pray for you on a continual basis! God bless you!

# FOREWORD BY DARRIN BALDWIN

Chris Musgrove has been a mentor and a personal friend of mine for over 30 years. I have experienced so many powerful moments with him along the way! While reading through some of the stories in this book, I had tears welling up in my eyes because I remembered being involved with so many of the events he described.

Chris personally reached out to me before I became a Christian. He showed me such love and kindness at a time when my life was at its lowest point. Chris and his wife Terri even opened up their home to me on two occasions. Their actions forever changed the course of my life and have made an eternal impact on me. Chris is one of the reasons I started serving Jesus! I wanted my life to look just like his. He had so much energy and excitement operating through him as he pursued God's plan for his life.

I have watched Chris go after people by doing large evangelistic campaigns, and I've also seen him leave the 99 to go after the one. I was one of the ones he personally went after, and his actions altered the course of my life. Chris is truly a people person. He lives for people. In a day and age where people are withdrawing more and more, Chris is RUNNING to where the people are!

Chris's story is one of faith, and one of God's tremendous favor. It's also about the life-changing power of Jesus! I hope this book touches and inspires you as much as it did for me. You won't regret taking the time to go on this journey of faith in God and learning about the birthing of FutureNow!

Blessings,

— *Darrin Baldwin*
*Pastor and Author, Melody Church,*
*Live Oak, FL*

## Foreword by Shellie Love

Have you ever wondered if one life can really matter? When I was younger, I always imagined my life counting! On the days when I had no friends over, I would be outside with my baseball bat in hand, and my imagination would kick in. A feeling would rise up within me that I was going to matter! I would cock the bat, while keeping my elbows up. At the plate, I would say, in a voice like it's projecting over stadium speakers, "Shellie Hancock is up to bat. It's the bottom of the ninth and bases are loaded with two outs." It would always be game four of the World Series. Not only was the game on the line, the entire series was as well. We were always down by one run.

As I gazed at the imaginary pitcher, the pitch would come in. I would swing, hit the ball, and slowly run around the bases. Throwing my hands in the air, I would imagine hearing the cheer of the crowd in the stands, as the ball would soar over the fence. In that moment, I felt like I had just done something really great!

As I grew older, that desire never left. I always wanted my life to count for something. It wasn't until I was a teenager that I began to understand what it was that my life was meant to be. I discovered that it actually could count and not just in an imaginary world.

As I was growing up in Live Oak, Florida, I didn't even understand the impact that was being made by Chris and Terri Musgrove, my youth pastors. The crazy thing is that as a teenager, their actions and roles just seemed like ordinary, day-to-day interactions. I didn't realize that what I had in my life is what most teenagers never have. I didn't have just youth leaders or even youth pastors. I had MENTORS, people who walked beside me day in and day out. Through good and bad, they believed in me no matter what.

No, they weren't perfect. In fact, all of us who have grown up under their ministry as teenagers, have joked about writing a book entitled, *101 Ways Not To Do Youth Ministry*. What they did was nothing magical or spectacular, but it was impactful. They had no boundaries with their love. It reached you, no matter what place you were in life, but most importantly it was consistent. They both embodied the heart of God for this generation. They were willing to live vulnerably and honestly, with a heart of love and an incredible passion for their heavenly Father's call to change a generation.

I could tell you more stories than this entire book could contain about the author. Some would have you rolling on the floor laughing. Others would have you in disbelief, while a few would make you cry. All would be true. However, the one thing I am completely certain of is that because of Chris Musgrove, my life's trajectory was shifted for the better and for eternity!

I've always said the greatest mistake the devil made was that he did not understand just how far God's love would go! I believe this is also true of Chris. After you meet him you never forget him. He opens his entire world up to you. If you allow it, he will take your entire world into his. It is such an example of The Great Exchange! His family becomes your family and your family becomes his. I'll never forget the services, the mission trips, the youth van trips with the drama team, or making chocolate chip cookies at 1 a.m. These days turned into years of walking together and learning from him how to love people and to go the distance with them in a way that gives opportunity for a changed life!

Let me set the stage for where we are now. If you have your finger on the pulse of this world on any level, you already know the state of the teenage population. Also, I'm sure you have heard the numerous statistics concerning young people and their relationship with God and the church.

I believe this world is in its final hours. But there is a generation rising up that knows only one thing. They are convinced that God does deliver, sets people free, and He will do it right NOW! There are people just like Chris and Terri all over the world who have given their lives to walk the school halls and enter homes while no one sees them or honors what they do. But, one life at a time, these amazing servants are

31

changing the culture in a generation and mobilizing an army for end-time evangelism.

In this book, you will read about the transition in Chris and Terri's life from almost 20 years of youth ministry to a nationally known ministry, called FutureNow. Their ministry has extended into public schools and is touching countless lives. Entire cities are impacted by each event! Propelled by obedience, they simply kept saying yes to what God asked them to do.

Now, they find themselves standing hand in hand, with their own children on the frontlines evangelizing a generation that the world has given up on. FutureNow is one of the best and only ministries that I know to the teens within the public schools. Their impact on young people is as effective as it is innovative.

If you are looking for a model of how to reach teenagers, seeking to be inspired by an army of young people that are being raised up in America, or you just want to read a story about a life that mattered, then this is your book. When it seems that our youth are losing the biggest battles they have ever faced, God has strategically placed people like Chris Musgrove up to bat!

What you hold in your hands is not just a book, it's a life. It's a story about a life that not only counted but has possibly made the single greatest impact on my life and countless others. So, I have one question for you. Are you willing to make the sacrifices to engage in God's plan for you to matter in the lives of the people around you?

I pray this book inspires you and encourages you to make your days matter, and that you can learn from the passion of the man who still impacts my life today. You are never too young to start, and never too old to press on.

> *— Shellie Hancock Love*
> *Youth Pastor and Missionary Evangelist,*
> *Millennial Church, Tulsa, OK*

# INTRODUCTION

I made Jesus the Lord of my life in 1981 by praying a prayer that I read in the back of a Kenneth E. Hagin mini-book. It was a book my brother, Steve, left in my apartment. Thank God somebody thought enough of me to leave a message of hope that could bring about change in my life. That prayer set my life on a course of faith in God and His plan for my life.

Life with God is a faith adventure filled with giving, loving, and serving. But it requires complete and instant obedience to God.

Jeremiah 29:11 says, "For I know the thoughts that I think toward you, says the Lord, thoughts of peace and not of evil, to give you a future and a hope." God is thinking about you; He has a plan for you; and He has gifted you to carry out that plan. It is your purpose! Until you discover the purpose for your existence, you're simply existing. I call it "drifting" or aimless living. Proverbs 29:18 says, "Without a vision, my people perish." I tell teenagers, "If you don't know where you're going, you'll take every road."

This book, *Journey to My FutureNow*, is my story of finding my purpose, gifting, and, most importantly, my place as a child of God and a joint heir with Jesus Christ.

Now more than ever people are longing for fulfillment of purpose. I believe this book will help anyone, at any place in life, to begin to step out on God's plan and purpose for them. I strongly encourage you to read the "What Others Are Saying" section, written by my fellow ministers and friends who read early drafts of this book. Their words will help build expectancy in you to receive all that God has for you as you read my story! Truly, most of these individuals were a big part of my journey.

Ask the Holy Spirit to begin to reveal the next step in God's plan and purpose for your life and step out in the faith-adventure, future, and hope that God has for you!

— *Chris Musgrove*

# CONTENTS

In Loving Memory of
Bobbie Jean Musgrove
11/25/1989 - 6/22/2020


R. A. "Rusty" Griffin
Former Chairman of the Board – FutureNow
8/22/1944 - 11/5/2019


Joe H. Anderson Jr.
Friend and Ministry Partner
7/10/1939 - 11/29/2016

CHAPTER ONE

# The Beginning

In the spring of 1990, I had the pleasure of meeting Steve McHargue. Steve is the Area Director of the Fellowship of Christian Athletes for North Central Florida.

He asked me if I would be willing to help facilitate an in-school assembly program in various schools within a four-county area of North Central Florida, which included Hamilton, Lafayette, Madison, and Suwannee counties.

For six years, I had been serving as a youth pastor at Melody Church in Live Oak. Steve knew about my work with youth and wanted my help in planning, organizing, and promoting the events.

I had grown up in that same North Florida area and knew lots of people in every one of the communities that he wanted to reach. Without hesitation, I accepted his offer to help!

Steve was interested in finding motivational speakers for both the day-time assemblies. To help him do that, I contacted a friend of mine, Fairest Hill, a Christian singer who attended the same Bible school I had and had ministered at our church several times.

Fairest suggested Joseph Jennings, a nationally recognized motivational speaker, as they had worked together to hold school assemblies in the past.

They both were available and agreed to come, so we went to work scheduling the assemblies with the schools in the area. My role at these in-school assemblies was to transport Fairest and Joseph to each school, connect with the school administrators, ensure the venue was set up correctly, and test the sound system and other equipment needed.

At each assembly program, Fairest Hill would open with rap songs to boost excitement and the involvement of the students. Joseph would then follow by telling his story.

Joseph Jennings reminded me a lot of Mr. T, a character from the *A-Team*, a 1980s television program, and the *Rocky III* movie! Joseph grew up in the inner city of South Bend, Indiana, where he was involved with gangs, violence, and everything else that accompanied that lifestyle. He grew up on the streets and made many wrong choices in his life, involving drugs, crime, and sex. He almost lost his life multiple times due to gunfire and stabbing.

When he gave his life to Christ, he started sharing his testimony with others and had a "tremendous desire to see the salvation of both young and old." He was an in-your-face, intimidating speaker. At one assembly, he shouted to a student who was talking and not paying attention, "Get up and get out, or I will throw you out!"

The student quickly got up and left. There was no more talking after that; Joseph had their full attention! In just four days, May 1-4, 1990, we held 15 different in-school assembly programs in five different high schools, two elementary schools, and two junior high schools within those four counties. The focus of all 15 assemblies was, "You can be a winner over drugs, alcohol, absenteeism, failure, etc."

In addition to the in-school assemblies, on Friday night, May 4th at 7:00 p.m. we scheduled an area-wide evangelistic rally to be held in Live Oak, Florida at the Suwannee County Coliseum.

The students and their families were invited to attend the rally by the student-members of the Fellowship of Christian Athletes Club (FCA) in each school.

I still have a letter dated April 17, 1990 that we received from A. P. Nott, the mayor of Live Oak at that time. In that letter he proclaimed the week of April 30th - May 4th, 1990, as "You Can Be a Winner Week" in preparation for the meetings.

This proclamation was made to help promote the event in the community. He even requested that the rental fee for the Suwannee County Coliseum be waived for the rally.

The community support for these events helped tremendously. Faith in God for our event was high, but we had no idea if anyone would come back to the outreach that night. We had done everything we knew to prepare.

We were thinking maybe a few hundred students would show up on Friday night. To our surprise, an estimated 2,200 people were in attendance, about one-fourth of the entire population of the city of Live Oak!

Several of the communities even arranged to bus their students to the event. We had a packed house! We had prayed, planned, worked hard, and now we were about to see the fruit of all our labor. Everything paid off because Joseph's message got through!

After Joseph shared his story about the life-changing power of Jesus Christ, he gave an invitation for the attendees to change their lives forever and 400 people came forward to receive Jesus Christ as Lord!

It was the most remarkable thing I had ever seen! Many of the churches in our four-county area did not even have 400 people attending their services regularly. Yet in one night, 400 people made commitments to follow Christ: Glory to God!

## CHAPTER TWO

# Passion Ignited

Seeing those 400 people make decisions for Jesus was like a fire inside me (Jeremiah 20:9), which nothing could extinguish. Something alive entered my heart and grabbed hold of it.

At the time, I didn't know what I now know about vision. I just knew that I had to do whatever it took to repeat what had taken place that night. I remember thinking, "If this can happen in Live Oak, Florida, it can happen anywhere!"

The passion for the salvation of students that God ignited in me that night would keep me awake at night and get me out of bed in the morning.

I believe the greatest test of a God-given passion within your heart is when it is all you can think and talk about; it consumes you.

For the mouth speaks what the heart is full of. (Matthew 12:34 NIV)

For years after that outreach program, I shared my passion with anyone who would listen, including friends, relatives, pastors, and missionaries.

Sometimes people would ask, "So, Chris, when are you going to do this?"

I would react with, "I don't have a story like Joseph Jennings." After all, I have never been a gang member, shot, or stabbed. I've never been to prison or almost died in a car wreck. I didn't think my story would stir students to relate, respond, and want to change their lives.

However, what I did have was a passion for reaching students for Jesus! I didn't know how or when to turn my passion into a reality, but I knew God was up to something. If I trusted Him, I was confident that He would bring it to pass when the time was right.

The Power Team was popular around that time. They were the Christian superstars of the 1980s.

During their programs in schools and mega-churches, these former athletes and body-builders would bust concrete blocks, tear large phone books in half, and break baseball bats, all while preaching the Gospel. I would tell people that I couldn't even break an old rake handle, much less a baseball bat!

But I knew there was something I was supposed to do; I just didn't know how. I was learning to be patient, trusting in God, and walking in faith, not by sight, as we are instructed to in II Corinthians 5:7 (KJV).

In waiting to hear from God, I studied Scripture, consulted respected Christian leaders, and prayed without ceasing. Drawn to God's teaching about vision in Habakkuk 2:2-3, I loved how the different translations of the Scripture encouraged me in my time of waiting.

> Then the Lord answered me and said, "Write the vision and engrave it plainly on [clay] tablets so that the one who reads it will run. For the vision is yet for the appointed [future] time. It hurries toward the goal [of fulfillment]; it will not

fail. Even though it delays, wait [patiently] for it, because it will certainly come; it will not delay." (AMP)

Then the Lord answered me and said, "Write the vision, and make it plain upon tables, that he may run that readeth it. For the vision is yet for an appointed time, but at the end it shall speak, and not lie: though it tarry, wait for it; because it will surely come, it will not tarry." (Habakkuk 2:2-3 KJV)

Many years ago, I heard a pastor speaking on a passage from Luke 1:39-45 describing Mary, the pregnant mother of Jesus, visiting Elizabeth. At Mary's greeting, Elizabeth's babe leaped in her womb. After reading those verses, he asked the question, "What makes your baby jump?"

I could relate to that expression! I liked it so much that I added it to the explanation of my passion and purpose:

"It is what keeps you awake at night and what gets you out of bed every morning. It is what makes your baby jump!"

I knew there was something God had for me to do because it was so strong on the inside of me, growing just like that babe in Elizabeth's womb.

But again, I had to be patient and wait for the appointed time.

I am beginning to understand why God doesn't show us in advance where we are going or how we will get there or how long it will take. If we knew where it would take us or how much we had to go through to get there and how long it would take, we might not follow through.

However, take joy in knowing that God has a plan for you!

It is a process – with steps to take and lessons to learn – in completing that plan, there will be no shortcuts.

If Joseph, the dreamer, would have known or seen in advance all the things he had to face and all the things that would happen to him before he became second in command in Egypt, he may have opted out of God's dreams and plans!

Proverbs 4:18 has always helped strengthen my faith during those periods of waiting and transition … the times when I don't know precisely where the path is or in what direction it will take me.

> But the path of the just is like the shining sun, that shines ever brighter unto the perfect day. (Proverbs 4:18)

> The way of the righteous is like morning light that gets brighter and brighter till it is full day. (Proverbs 4:18 CEB)

I held on to that passion for students that God dropped in my heart and patiently waited as things began to get brighter and brighter.

What better example of trusting God than of Mary in Luke 2:19?

> But Mary kept all these things and pondered them in her heart. (Luke 2:19)

Then two years later …

## CHAPTER THREE

# Are You Willing?

In the summer of 1992, my wife, Terri, and I received a call from a representative from a student foreign exchange program looking for host homes for their students. As youth pastors, the organization hoped we might know of someone from our church who might be interested in hosting a student.

They told us of a young man, Danny Stanik, from Czechia, also known as the Czech Republic, who had been assigned a host family and was on his way to the U.S. However, at the very last minute, the host family changed their mind and backed out of the agreement.

I could sense by the tone of her voice that the representative was desperately seeking a host home for this young man. When I told my wife about the situation, she asked, "Why don't we take him?"

I hadn't thought of that but, "Why not?"

Danny Stanik joined our family, and he became like an older brother to my five-year-old daughter, Kasey, and my two-year-old son, Christian. When the school year ended, there were lots of tears when we had to put Danny on the plane back to the Czech Republic.

A few months after Danny went home, the Stanik family invited us to visit the Czech Republic to thank us for hosting their son. They wired the funds needed, and we arranged to take vacation time from work. It was January 1994, and we were off on our first trip to Europe; we were extremely excited.

Danny and his family lived in Prague, the capital city of the Czech Republic. What a beautiful city it was, with its cathedrals and castles! We also visited Germany and Austria because the countries are so close to Czechia.

Everything was incredibly beautiful, and we felt blessed with the opportunity God had provided.

However, while enjoying the beauty of all that surrounded us, we became increasingly aware of the large population of gypsies living in Prague. Our hearts were drawn to them as we saw them daily roaming up and down the streets and gathered in groups on the busy street corners. There were large groups of them everywhere you looked.

I found myself asking, "What's going to happen to all these people?"

The reply I received from someone familiar with their plight shocked me. The answer he gave was, "Well, according to your belief system, they are all going to hell."

With that one shocking statement, an intense burden for them dropped into our hearts, as well as for the Czech Republic.

It was far more than just feeling sorry for them. I am telling you, we both had a powerful desire to be there, in Czechia, to bring the good news to these people.

I remembered hearing Rick Renner, a missionary pastor to Moscow, explaining how he immediately felt after he announced he was moving his family from the United States to the Soviet Union. He really hoped everyone he consulted would tell him not to go. But his pastor, close friends, and even his own children said they should go. After he made his official announcement concerning the move, he said that he became physically sick to the point of throwing up!

We felt sick to our stomachs when we contemplated what this would mean for our lives and our family in the natural, especially when we talked about where our children would attend school when we moved there. But we knew that no matter how we felt, we would obey God.

Returning to Florida, we had to act on this leading in our spirits that we had received. The first thing we thought to do was to contact Rhema Bible College, where I had graduated. We enquired about any connections that they may have to the Czech Republic.

The school gave us the name of Larry and Angela Keaton, missionaries in Prague. Angela happened to be one of my instructors when I attended college in the mid-1980s.

I telephoned the Keaton family and introduced myself. I shared with them the intense burden for the lost that we had experienced during our visit to the Czech Republic. Larry advised that if I was serious, I should come back for a second visit. That way, I could "spy out the land," so to speak.

We made the arrangements for me to return to Prague and meet with Larry and Angela. It was expensive to fly to Europe. We did not have the extra money for me to go. However, Terri and I knew we needed to obey the leading of the Holy Spirit. We sold my truck to pay for the trip.

I loved that truck, but it was a sacrifice that we were willing to make to be obedient to the Lord.

Back in the Czech Republic, Larry and Angela were great hosts. They invited me to their Bible study, and I was able to tour parts of the city Terri and I had not seen before. I even had the opportunity to revisit Danny and the Stanik family. The search for a house and schools for our children was next on my list during my week-long stay. That's how serious we were about the move.

During my time in the Czech Republic, I began to realize that I no longer felt that same intense desire to be there. The burden I had sensed so strong before wasn't there anymore.

It's difficult to explain, and it didn't make any sense to me. I called my wife and shared with her what was happening in my heart. I told Terri I was coming home.

For weeks, I wrestled in my mind as to why God gave us that burden in our hearts to go to the Czech Republic. Why would God put us through all the trouble of having to sell my truck, raise the money, and travel to the Czech Republic, only to show me that He did not want me to go?

There must be a reason, but I couldn't see it at the time.

We found out the Lord was preparing us for something more. We would come to understand that God did not want us to move to the Czech Republic, but He did want us to experience something while we were there. He wanted to enlarge our hearts and cultivate in them a deep longing to reach a people group that was much larger than we had ever imagined. He was opening our eyes to see a forgotten, often overlooked, commonly believed to be unreachable people group.  A lost "population within a population" if you will.

Before this experience, we had sincerely loved the students in our own small fellowship of believers, and we had even begun to reach out to the students in our local community.

But God was preparing us to open our eyes and hearts and to see the population of the public-school system as a people group who were very much like the gypsies in the Czech Republic. They are often overlooked, forgotten, and believed to be unreachable with the gospel.

The vast number of American school kids are, for twelve years, simply passing through the hallways and hanging out at the corners and fringes of our public school system and a "population within a population."

God was also testing our willingness to leave what we had, our homes, our comfortable ministry, our family and friends, and like Abraham, go to a place that he would show us (Gen 12:1).

I believe we passed the test. When the time came for us to step out in full-time ministry with Future Now, we would be willing!

But there was more for us to learn before we continued on our journey.

CHAPTER FOUR

# Brighter and Brighter

From 1994 until 1998, we continued to faithfully serve in our local church and minister to the youth in our community, but the heart of our ministry was decisively more focused on outreach.

Our Christian concerts grew larger, our community dramas more intense, our mission trips with the youth more frequent, and our youth group was growing. Our church invested in a radio station, so we took to the airwaves, and then they purchased a bus that helped start a bus ministry. Working with the local football coach, I became the chaplain of the high school team in 1997.

That same year we launched "Club 180." Club 180 was a Christian clubhouse or hangout where teenagers could come on Friday and Saturday nights. We had arcade games, pool tables, a stage for bands, drama teams, or speakers who would perform or minister most nights that we were open. Club 180 was a place for young people to gather, invite their friends, and turn their lives around, heading them into a new direction; thus, a "180-degree" turn around.

In the fall of 1997, I got a telephone call from Shellie Hancock Love, a former student from my youth group, one of my more active members I might add, who had gone on to Bible school and was currently working with a ministry out of Tulsa Oklahoma, Shekinah Glory.

They had received requests from two different pastors who they knew in England and Scotland for a youth ministry team from the United States to come to England and Scotland and minister to their youth. If we were interested and were in a position to take a group of youth overseas, they would pass our names on to these pastors in Europe!

Yes, we were definitely interested!

The youth band and drama team that we had put together in our local church led praise and worship in other churches, at youth camps, the local Fellowship of Christian Athletes' meetings, and any other door that the Lord would open for us.

With the experience we gained in presenting music and drama to youth in our local area, I felt that the team was ready to make the trip to Europe.

In the fall of 1997, we contacted Pastor Di Stacey in Liverpool, England and Pastor Bernie McLaughlin of Kilwinning, Scotland, and set the dates. We were off to the United Kingdom in June of 1998.

My wife, Terri, and I, along with one youth leader and nine team members landed in Manchester, England, and rented a van. It was a little nerve-racking for our team because the steering wheel was on the passenger side, and it was a stick shift. If that was not enough, I had to adjust to driving on the wrong side of the road! Miraculously, with my driving, we had no accidents.

In preparing for our first trip to the United Kingdom (UK), people warned us that ministering in the UK would be a challenge. We found that warning to be all too true. In one of the meetings, I remember having 120 students in attendance, and only one person knew John 3:16.

In the United States, almost everyone can quote that Scripture. You could ask a prostitute in New York City and she would probably know John 3:16.

None of those students or their families attended church regularly. Only a handful of students even admitted to attending church at Christmas with their grandparents. Most of the churches were closed because the older adults who had attended had died. With the following generations not attending church, there was no one left. A church with 100 members was considered a megachurch in the UK.

Our first stop was in Liverpool, England. We ministered at Grace Family Church during their Sunday morning service. The following week, we ministered in the streets, parks, or anywhere we found people gathered. We invited everyone we saw to a church service. Even though we passed out fliers and reached out to many people, we barely had a response to our invitations.

While we were there, Pastor Dianna Stacey arranged for us to visit a local school and present our program during a school assembly. Pastor Stacey informed the Headmaster of the school that we were a Christian group. She made sure he knew that our music, drama presentations, and messages were from a Christian perspective.

He said he understood and insisted that we hold the assembly. He told us we could even make a plea or bid to the students if we liked. In other words, we could invite the students to make commitments to Jesus Christ through an altar call or invitation. After he assured us there would not be a problem with our message, we agreed to hold the assembly.

It was the team's very first time performing for an assembly program at a school, much less one in England! We had served at baccalaureate ceremonies and school talent shows in the

United States, but never an assembly program during school hours.

When our team arrived at the school, we realized that it was a school for boys. Everyone wore their smart blue uniforms. We were also very excited to learn that John Lennon of the Beatles had attended this very school.

The assembly was a success! The several hundred students seemed thoroughly engaged in the music, drama, and message.

At the close of my presentation, I invited anyone who wanted to make a commitment to Jesus to come forward. One student got up out of his seat and walked down to meet me with tears streaming down his face.

What happened next caught me completely off guard. To my shock and dismay, the students began laughing at this young man as he made his way down the aisle.

Working with youth for the length of time that I had, I had witnessed a lot of crazy things in church services, but I had never seen anyone make fun of someone responding to an invitation to make Jesus Christ their Lord.

I was furious! I was sorely tempted to take off one of my shoes, throw it as hard as possible, and hope I hit someone in the face. I know that came from my flesh; thank God, I did not follow through on my natural inclinations.

But I did start shouting to get them to stop laughing. Once they became quiet, I did not have any idea what I was going to say next. Without thinking, I raised my voice and said, "They tell us that John Lennon attended this school, and that he stated that the Beatles would be more popular than Jesus Christ."

I did not have a clue why I said that. I was surprised that it even came out of my mouth. I had been told that John Lennon attended school there, but I did not know that he had made that statement. (I found out later he did.) I did not know where I was going with that statement, but God did.

I continued, "John Lennon is dead and still in his grave today, but Jesus Christ rose from His grave, and that's who this young man has come to receive today."

Never in my wildest dreams would I have imagined what would happen next. Two-thirds of those students who were just moments before laughing at their fellow classmate for his decision for Christ got up out of their seats and made their way to the front of the stage to join him. It was a glorious sight, and we were all in awe of what God had done! Yes, it was all God!

At the conclusion of that service, April (Sanchez) Perez, one of the young ladies on the outreach team, came up to me and practically begged, "Pastor Chris, when we get back to Florida, we've got to do this!"

Those words echoed the call God placed in my heart back in 1990. Unfortunately, I had to reply, "April, what we just did here is against the law in the state of Florida."

She responded, "But isn't there something we can do?"

I once again recalled the words of Habakkuk:

> For the vision is yet for an appointed time; But at the end *it will speak*, and it will not lie. Though it tarries, wait for it; because it will surely come, it will not tarry. (Habakkuk 2:3)

Here was my vision speaking to me through the mouths of my own youth group.

It had been seven years since God ignited this passion in my heart, but now the flame was growing brighter and brighter.

> … the path of the righteous is like the light of dawn, that shines brighter and brighter until the full day. (Proverbs 4:18 ESV)

CHAPTER FIVE

# Strengthened by Prophecy

But the one who prophesies speaks to people for their strengthening, encouraging, and comfort. (I Corinthians 14:3 NIV)

But when a person speaks what God has revealed, he speaks to people to help them grow, to encourage them, and to comfort them. (I Corinthians 14:3 GW)

In August of 1999, my daughter Kasey and I went to the Kingdom Bound Christian Music Festival at Six Flags Theme Park in Darien Lake, New York. I was there to meet with the directors of Kingdom Bound Ministries about helping them establish a Christian music festival in North Florida.

As I sat there, I began to second guess my decision to fly to New York. Terri was back home alone with our other three children, including our youngest son Isaac who was barely two months old. I was exhausted, missing my family, and feeling out of place as if I missed God.

As I look back, I realize now that the enemy was working behind the scenes to discourage me. Little did the enemy know that God was about to bless me with supernatural strength, encouragement, and comfort.

I remember it like it was yesterday. As I was struggling with these discouraging thoughts, the worship service was beginning. Darlene Zschech and the Hillsong band started singing, "Shout to the Lord."

Words cannot describe how anointed this worship service was. I was blessed to be there as a guest of Kingdom Bound Ministries and to be in what I thought was reserved seating right at the front of the stage.

At one point, I thought the rapture would occur in the glory of that united worship to God! I really needed it!

As I was soaking all this in, I noticed an usher heading straight towards me. It was then that I realized I wasn't in the reserved section after all, but was sitting in the reserved handicapped seating section. I was prepared to make my apologies and move to another seat if necessary, but before I could say a word, she put her hand on my shoulder and spoke these words to me, "My son, I will help you make that move you are going to make. I will help you reach that generation I have called you to reach, and I will give you songs in the night."

Then she turned and walked away. I was in complete awe. Here I was feeling discouraged, second-guessing myself, and afraid of being booted from the meeting, and God sends a volunteer usher to give me a word of prophecy to strengthen and encourage me.

God is good, and He has an awesome sense of humor!

Later that night, when we were catching the shuttle to our hotel in Buffalo, we were blessed to ride with Darlene Zschech. She laid hands on me and prayed in that strong Aussie accent a powerful prayer that I will not soon forget.

Again I was strengthened, encouraged, and comforted. I knew God had me right where He wanted me. He gave me an encouraging word to cause me to continue to fight for my vision.

> This charge I commit to you, son Timothy, according to the *prophecies previously made concerning you*, that by them you may wage the good warfare. (I Timothy 1:18)

In other words, when the devil tries to tell you that you will never accomplish what God has called you to do. You can be encouraged, strengthened, and comforted by the prophecies that are spoken over you and continue to fight the good fight of faith.

In 2001, eleven years after the initial vision was dropped in my heart in Live Oak at the Joseph Jennings event, we held our first U.S. in-school assembly program at Suwannee High School in Live Oak, Florida.

I personally did not want our first program to be held there. It was where I went to high school. There were teachers at that school who knew me a little too well; some of them had even graduated with me! The principal jokingly told me that one of the teachers said, "I cannot believe that Chris Musgrove is speaking to our students."

We were originally scheduled to hold an assembly in Hamilton County, but it was cancelled. That was where I wanted to start, because no one at that school knew me. My reasoning was that, "If we bombed, no one I knew would know."

Having heard about our cancellation, the principal at Suwannee High School, Clyde Sperring, invited us to do a pre-prom assembly with the high school students. We had not held a school assembly program since England. In Liverpool, the program consisted of Christian music, dramas, and teaching.

For the public-school assembly in Florida, we had to change our music and drama presentations to a non-Christian, motivational

Joseph Jennings speaking to a group of students

Chris in Prague, Czech Republic with Zolt Stanik & Danny Stanik, exchange student, in 1993

Chris and Terri on the crowded streets of Prague, Czech Republic

**In 1998, Melody Church Youth Group on mission trip to Liverpool, England**

Team ministering at an all boys school in Liverpool, England.

In 1998, team ministering in Scotland

**First Future Now assembly at
Suwannee High School in Live Oak, FL in 2001**

FutureNow's first stadium event at Lowndes High School in 2006

FN team in 2006

In 2013, Chris at an event praying over the students

Chris, at an evening event, sharing Romans 10:9-10 with students at the altar, in 2015

FN team in 2016

In 2017, students at an evening event, making Jesus Lord of their lives

Video presentation using LED wall at FutureNow event in 2018

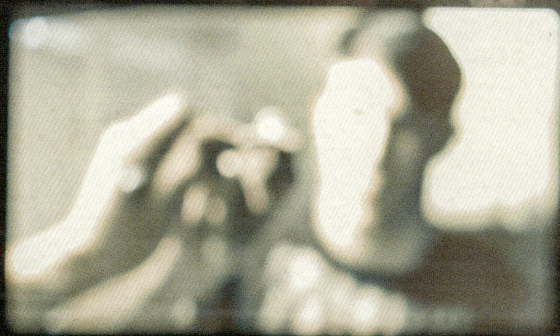

A powerful drama at a FN assembly in 2019

The Musgrove Family in June 2020

theme. Then, after the assembly, a student-led Christian club active on the campus planned to invite students to come back that night to a Christian music concert where we could present an evangelistic outreach.

The night before, as I was preparing for this program, I was experiencing feelings of anxiety, fear, and inadequacy. I had no previous experience holding a motivational school assembly.

As a youth pastor, I was especially concerned that I would mention the name of God, or Jesus, or quote scripture like I usually do when speaking to youth.

In addition, it was Suwannee High School! It was my home town, the school I graduated from, and in front of some of my former teachers!

This attack of fear and anxiety was so strong that it made me feel physically sick and caused me to again second guess myself.

As I was looking through some notes preparing for the next day's assembly program, I came across these words that I had written in my journal precisely one year earlier in April 2000:

> *As I was praying today, the Holy Spirit spoke to me and said, "One year from now, you will be going into the public schools to do an assembly program."*

Reading these words of prophecy written in my own handwriting flooded my soul with the peace of God, along with a boldness that I had never known. My fear, anxiety, and feelings of inadequacy disappeared. I knew God was with me. He had gone before me.

I knew the assembly would be a total success. Why? Because God had spoken these promises to me a year earlier, and He was bringing it all to pass.

That is the purpose of prophecy! To strengthen, to encourage, and to comfort. I was now fearless to face those students.

> Those who prophesy speak to people, building them up and giving them

> encouragement and comfort. (I Cor. 14:3 CEB)

> The prophetic word that was directed to you prepared us for this. All those prayers are coming together now, so you will do this well, *fearless in your struggle*, keeping a firm grip on your faith and on yourself. (I Timothy 1:18 MSG)

> If God be for us who can be against us. (Romans 8:31b KJV)

The next day, as they opened the curtains in that high school auditorium, I walked out on the stage and yelled out, "Hallel … How are you doing?"

I caught myself before I finished saying "Hallelujah!" Fortunately, I don't think anyone noticed.

Our first assembly program lasted about an hour. We played music, performed dramas, and had students share stories of how they turned their lives around by making better choices.

After the assembly, the students were invited by the Fellowship of Christian Athletes to a Youth Rally that night. More than 300 students returned to attend the concert, and 30 students made commitments to Jesus Christ. It was the open door we had been waiting for!

Several weeks later, another word of prophecy heightened the sense of urgency within me. Close friends of ours, Charles and Angie Neeley, invited a couple from Lake City, Florida, to come to church with them. The wife of the visiting couple came to me after the service and handed me a thin piece of folded paper. She had torn off the edge of her church bulletin and written a note on it.

When I unfolded her note, in small print, were the words:

> *"The longer you wait, the less people you'll reach."*

She told me she had no idea what it meant, but God had told her to give it to me. It was time to step out!

That summer, July 2001, we set up a nonprofit organization called Chris Musgrove Ministries Incorporated to do just that. We needed a name for our in-school assembly program. I wanted it to be a name with significant scriptural meaning, but one that would not be inappropriate in the public-school setting.

A family member suggested the name FutureNow when he heard of the message we planned on sharing.

I liked it for two reasons. First, it fully embodied the message of "making right choices today for your success in the future" that we delivered in the daytime school assemblies. Secondly, and most importantly, it expressed an even deeper scriptural idea.

> "For I know the plans I have for you," declares the LORD, "plans to prosper you and not to harm you, plans to give you hope and a future. (Jeremiah 29:11 NIV)

> Because Jesus was raised from the dead, we've been given a brand-new life and

have everything to live for, including a future in heaven – and the future starts now! (I Peter 1:3-5 MSG)

CHAPTER SIX

# Kill the Cow, Burn the Plow

About one year later, while still serving as a youth pastor in Live Oak, I received a phone call from Judy Sumrall. Judy was from Cross City, Florida, and had been a member of our church since it began. She taught school at Dixie County High School in Cross City, Florida.

Judy had heard about the success of our school assembly program in Live Oak so she sought permission from her high school principal to invite us to hold a program at her school. They agreed and we were scheduled for an event on April 8th, 2002.

While we were in the Dixie County High School Auditorium and setting up for the assembly program, I received a phone call from the Lighthouse Christian Center in Mayo, Florida. The board members wanted to know if I would consider becoming an interim pastor at their church.

In my mind, the answer was "no," but something about the word "interim" caught my attention. Interim means temporary and I knew that we were in a place of transition, so I agreed to pray about it.

After praying, my wife and I both believed that we were supposed to take the job as the interim pastor.

Leaving Melody Church, after being a youth pastor there for seventeen years, was not an easy thing for several reasons! First and foremost, I had been a member of the church for over twenty years, from the time I gave my life to Christ while in college. Secondly, we had just completed a brand-new youth facility that took years to plan and build. We had only been in that building one year.

It was even tougher to leave because I was acting as chaplain for the Suwannee High School football team. Since 1997, I worked with Jay Walls, the new football coach at the school.

For five years, this chaplain position enabled me to be more involved with students than ever.

So why would we leave now? Even though it did not make sense yet, Terri and I were determined to follow God's voice in obedience to what we had heard.

> My sheep hear my voice, I know them, and they follow me. (John 10:27)

Once I resigned to take the interim position in Mayo, Pastor Frank asked me, "You are coming back, right?"

I couldn't give him an answer. We loved Pastor Frank and Amanda Davis, our church, and serving as youth pastors.

As I said before, it was difficult even to consider leaving. However, we knew the next step was to become interim pastors at Lighthouse Christian Center until God showed us the next step.

I have never had the Lord show me or tell me anything for more than a few years out. In other words, I needed more light or revelation (revealing) to see beyond the interim position that we had taken. You can only see as far as the light will shine. The light comes from God. It also comes from His Word.

> God is light, and in Him is no darkness at all. (I John 1:5)

> Your word is a lamp to my feet and a light to my path. (Psalm 119:105)

I could see where I was now (my feet) and where I was to go next (my path). The light of God's word and direction shines out along the way to illuminate our path, step by step.

During the transition from Live Oak to Mayo, a fellow minister, Pastor David Stephens, called to say, "The Lord told me to tell you to kill the ox and burn the plow. I am not exactly sure what that means, but I'm supposed to tell you that."

That same day my wife came home from a weekend women's conference and said the guest speaker had given her the message: "Kill the ox and burn the plow."

> For to one is given the word of wisdom
> through the Spirit. (I Corinthians 12:8a)

That was a word of wisdom, one of the nine gifts of the Spirit mentioned in I Corinthians 12, that was working through my friend. That same gift was also working through a speaker at a women's conference to give my wife the same scripture. God had confirmed through two witnesses our future direction. We would not be returning to Melody.

> …by the mouth of two or three witnesses
> the matter shall be established.
> (Deuteronomy 19:15b)

The scripture concerning "killing the ox and burning the plow" is found in I Kings and reads:

> So he departed from there and found
> Elisha the son of Shaphat, while he was
> plowing with twelve pairs of oxen before
> him, and he with the twelfth. And Elijah
> passed over to him and threw his mantle
> on him. He left the oxen and ran after
> Elijah, and said, "Please let me kiss my
> father and my mother, then I will follow

you." And he said to him, Go back again, for what have I done to you? So he [Elisha] returned from following him, and took the pair of oxen and sacrificed them and boiled their flesh with the implements of the oxen, and gave it to the people and they ate. Then he arose and followed Elijah and ministered to him. (I Kings 19:19-21 NAS)

When presented with the chance to become Elijah's assistant, Elisha at once said "Yes." Elisha's only request was that he be able to bid goodbye to his parents. Elijah allowed him and, at the same time, released Elisha from any obligation.

This word from the Lord was a release for us from our assignments at Melody, our youth group, and our involvement in Suwannee High School. We were free to step out.

At the same time that we were planning our departure, Darrin Baldwin, one of my former youth leaders, a drummer in our youth band, and son-in-law of Pastor Frank, called his father-in-law about wanting to move back to Live Oak.

He attended Rhema Bible Training College in Tulsa, Oklahoma, at the same time Pastor Frank's daughter, Laura, was also at Oral Roberts University in Tulsa. Darrin had been serving as a youth pastor at a church in New Jersey since graduating from Bible school.

Darrin, who was a spiritual son to Terri and me, was already familiar with most of the church's youth and would be a perfect fit to take over as a youth pastor.

The desire of my heart was to leave the youth ministry at Melody better than I found it. The Holy Spirit had given me a quote a few years before that said, "Success is not measured by what you're leaving to, but by what you're leaving behind."

I had actually submitted that quote to John Maxwell, pastor, author, speaker, and leadership guru at a conference of his that I attended. He used this quote in chapter 21 of his book, *The 21 Irrefutable Laws of Leadership*, where he talks about the law of legacy.

With great joy and freedom, we could now step into our future assignment without regret or concern for what we were leaving behind.

We had personally helped disciple and mentor the new youth pastor and helped prepare, plan, and build a fabulous youth facility for Darrin and Laura. We were leaving the youth ministry better than we found it.

With God's help, we had succeeded!

CHAPTER SEVEN

# Your Four Children Will Starve

We were Interim Pastors at Lighthouse Christian Center in Mayo, Florida, for two years, and loved it. As the church grew, we started a Christian school, paved the church parking lot, added portable classrooms, and bought a church van.

We loved pastoring and living in Mayo, Florida. I became great friends with the high school football coach, Joey Pearson, and I was again asked to be the chaplain for the local high school football team. Our kids were involved in the community youth sports leagues.

We genuinely connected with the people in Mayo and fell in love with our new community. It was an exciting time in our lives.

But because it was so great, I was in danger of allowing the "interim" assignment to become permanent. I loved being around old friends and meeting new people, so I became quite comfortable pastoring.

But as busy as we were as pastors of the church, we still found time to hold our school assembly programs. We held programs in seven different middle and high schools in those two years.

In the spring of 2004, my wife came home from another weekend women's conference where the topic for the weekend was passion. She asked me point-blank, "What's your passion?"

Without even having to think, I said my passion was to be conducting school assemblies full-time.

Terri challenged me by pointing out, "You cannot successfully pastor a church and successfully do FutureNow."

She was right, and I knew what I had to do. As much as we loved being pastors, my passion was to be in front of those students.

In the spring of 2004, we announced to the Lighthouse Christian Center leadership that we were stepping down as pastors to hold FutureNow assemblies on a full-time basis.

A few weeks before we resigned, someone felt it necessary to warn me that if I were to quit my job, my four children would starve to death.

It is already difficult enough to step out on your dreams without someone trying to trample all over them with words.

I want to make it clear we did not just quit our job foolishly without a plan. Although the weekly salaries would end, we already had quite a few monthly supporters committed to us, and several schools already booked. However, we still did not have enough pledged to cover our monthly bills at the time we resigned, but we knew God was saying to step out in faith and trust Him.

Friends who are missionaries and others with traveling ministries had warned me that the first year would be the toughest. One missionary friend told me not to plan for a big Christmas that first year.

However, I am here to tell you, the God that guides also provides! That doesn't mean there wouldn't be challenges or struggles. For instance, after we hired our very first employee for FutureNow, Bobby Hofer, we found ourselves facing a payday without any funds to cover his paycheck.

Bobby was a great employee, multi-talented, and willing to do whatever we asked. He was our band director, guitarist, videographer, and receptionist. He was willing to perform drama, janitorial, and lawn work. He was such a blessing to the ministry we didn't want to have to let him go.

My son, Christian, who was about 13 at the time, must have overheard my wife and I discussing our inability to meet our payroll obligation. He came into the room with his piggy bank and announced that he wanted to give it to us to help pay Bobby. His piggy bank held around $200.

My wife then remembered that she had a gift card for $100 to Red Lobster that someone had given us and offered that as well.

Bobby hesitantly received the money and the gift card with my assurance that it was God that directed our son and my wife to give to the ministry.

After that we were never short on payroll again! What a blessing to see for myself that God had not only called me and given me a vision for this ministry, but that he had imparted that same calling and vision to my whole family. We were all in!

Upon leaving the church, we moved back to Live Oak, Florida. Fortunately, we still owned a house there that we were renting out while we were serving as interim pastors in Mayo.

After we moved back to Live Oak, we went back to Melody Church. We were excited to be back around people we loved, but we felt so out of place. We remembered the Word from the Lord, "To kill the ox and burn the plow." We knew in our hearts that our time at Melody Church had come to an end. God was sending us somewhere else.

But where? We started driving to New Covenant Church in Valdosta, Georgia. I had ministered to the youth there and had lots of friends in the church.

In February of 2005, while at a minister's conference in Tulsa, Oklahoma, we caught a glimpse of where God was leading us. Pastor Kenneth W. Hagin had a word of wisdom for my wife and me. He ministered to us that God was about to help us make a move. He cautioned us that we were to be extremely sensitive to the Spirit of God so that we would not miss it.

Two months later, we received a phone call from someone who wanted to buy our house. My first response was, "Our house is not for sale." Immediately, I remembered that word of wisdom to be sensitive or I would miss it.

I told the prospective buyers that I would call them back in a few days.

> The spirit of a man is the lamp of the LORD, searching all the inner depths of his heart. (Proverbs 20:27)

> For as many as are led by the Spirit of God, these are sons of God. (Romans 8:14)

We drove to Valdosta, Georgia, and met with Pastor L.A. Joiner, the pastor of New Covenant Church. He put us in touch with a realtor. Within two weeks, we sold our house in Florida and bought a house in Valdosta, with neither home on the realty market.

A realtor will tell you that it is impossible. It may be impossible with man, but not where God is at work!

There is more to our house story that brings glory to God. Terri had been praying and believing for a five-bedroom house in Valdosta. As we were looking at homes, the prices for four- and five-bedroom homes seemed out of reach. My wife's desire was for each of our children to have a bedroom of their own.

As youth pastors, we were always offering kids a place to stay, which meant our kids continually had to share a bed or a bedroom. It was important to Terri to give that gift of space and privacy to each of our children.

She was standing on the word of God found in Ephesians:

> Now to Him who is able to do exceedingly abundantly above all that we ask or think, according to the power that works in us. (Ephesians 3:20)

As I took my concerns about our new home to the Lord in prayer, He informed me that my wife was in faith about this house. He said if I could not get in faith with her, I needed to let off the brakes and ride the clutch and let her pull me along with her faith.

I am here to tell you, I did just that, and God moved in a big way. We did not get a five-bedroom house. We got a six-bedroom home! He answered her prayers exceedingly abundantly above all that she could ask or think! Glory to God!!!

We moved to Valdosta in July of 2005. It was as if God was waiting for us to get there. The ministry was growing so fast that we needed help. God began supernaturally sending people to help us.

To start with, Rusty Griffin, a local businessperson, agreed to come on board as chairperson of our board of directors.

Not long after, we hired Brinson and Lori Barker of Lake City, Florida. Brinson was to be our community events coordinator and his wife, Lori, became our bookkeeper.

Originally from Valdosta, the couple was serving as youth pastors at Christian Heritage Church in Lake City. We first met them at an event we held at Columbia County High School in Lake City. They decided to attend another event that we held at Southeast Elementary School in Valdosta. We typically do not serve elementary schools, but Principal Alvin Hudson invited us, so we agreed to come. That day, 400 fifth-graders filled the gym for the event.

After the assembly, we invited the students and their families to our night event. We were overwhelmed by the turnout! Typical attendance for a night event is about sixty percent of the day time attendance.

In other words, if you see 1,000 students in a day assembly, a good turnout for the night event would be about 600. That night at Southeast Elementary, we had almost a 400 percent return on the day event! We had 400 students in attendance during the day and 1,500 who attended that night. It was a crazy and exciting night.

We were so very thankful that Brinson and Lori picked that particular night to attend another one of our events. Due to the overwhelming response that night, they both rolled up their sleeves and jumped in to help us pray and counsel with the large number of people who responded to the invitation.

After the event, they came to us and told us how their hearts were moved when they saw the number of people who were responding to the Lord in our FutureNow events and they knew we needed a team to be able to gather in a harvest of that size.

They had witnessed what I had that night in 1990 with Joseph Jennings. In fact, they were so amazed that they decided to move to Valdosta and serve with FutureNow, trusting God for the finances to be able to do so. They wanted to be a part of what they had seen the Lord accomplish that night at Southeast Elementary School.

Something else happened that night at Southeast Elementary! After the event, my youngest son, Isaac, and I were busy serving pizza and drinks to the 1,500 people who came that night. As you can imagine, it took us a while!

What's amazing about that night was that we only ordered enough pizza for 400 people, yet all 1,500 people came through the line and many came back after they ate their first slice to get in line for seconds.

Not only were we able to feed all 1,500 people there, there was even pizza left over for the FutureNow team to eat after everyone left.

We praise God for multiplying that pizza in our hands that night just like the fishes and loaves in the hands of the disciples.

When we were almost finished passing out the pizza, I noticed a woman standing by the gym door watching us. She was smiling like she wanted to talk to me. Very nicely dressed in a bright white outfit, I figured she was the principal's wife or possibly a school board member.

I asked if I could help her with something, and she responded, "You go ahead and finish what you are doing. I will wait, and when you are done, we can talk."

As soon as we finished, I walked over to her and asked her what I could do for her. She said she wanted to pray for all the FutureNow team members and asked me to round them up.

I explained it was almost impossible, as many were in the parking lot loading trucks or in the altar care room typing in names. Everyone was busy wrapping up for the night.

My son, Christian, and daughter, Kasey, were standing on the stage helping break down production equipment, so I motioned for them to come over to where we were. I told her, "This is probably the best I can do as far as getting the team together."

She replied, "That is great!" Then she explained she wanted to pray that God would fill us up for all we had done that night by pouring into the lives of all those students and their families.

Laying her hands on Kasey and then Christian, she began to prophesy things that God would do in their lives. Then she laid her hands on me and said that God was sending the 200 million dollars that I needed to do all that God had called me to do. When she said that, I thought she might as well have said two trillion dollars, but I sensed the anointing of God on her, as did my children.

Through the years I have often thought about that night and her words. To reach all fifty states and the uttermost parts of the world, 200 million dollars would just get us started.

Later that night, some of the team members asked about the woman who had prayed for us because they wanted her to pray for them as well. I went to the principal and asked him if he knew who the woman was waiting by the gym door. I described her, white dress, etc., but he said he didn't know who I was talking about. He never saw her.

One of our team members joked that she must have been an angel. Maybe she was! We have never had food multiply like that since, and that word about God sending 200 million dollars has bolstered my faith whenever we need to believe God for extra finances.

Within that first year in Valdosta, we had seven full-time employees. We were growing by leaps and bounds. However, our income was not. We were all trusting God for supernatural provision.

One day we received a call from a very successful businessperson I had recently met. He wanted to schedule a meeting with the chairman of the board of directors, the bookkeeper, and director of FutureNow.

Just a few weeks before this fateful call, we did not even have a chairperson, a board, or a bookkeeper! God supplied our needs just in time.

After he met with Rusty, Lori, and myself, he told me he would like to give FutureNow enough money to fund us for a full year. Glory to God!

It was enough to help us to take care of our ministry and the people God had sent us.

Not only did my four children not starve to death, but God supplied the funds to take care of a team of seven employees.

God is faithful, exceedingly abundantly above all that we could ask or think.

CHAPTER EIGHT

# The FutureNow Assembly: The Message

That same year we were in Nashville, Georgia, at Berrien County High School for a FutureNow assembly program. I was sharing real-life stories of students I have met over my seventeen years as a youth pastor. Stories about kids making either thoughtless decisions which ruined their lives in one split second, resulting in death, prison sentences, etc. or some that made wise decisions that had turned their lives completely around resulting in success.

While I was speaking, several students to my right, about four rows back, began laughing. They were becoming loud enough to bother me though I am not usually distracted by the crowd's noise.

This time it was different. Instead of becoming angry, I got emotional. I began to cry.

The only way I can describe what happened to me in that moment was that the compassion of God came over me for those young people. His concern and compassion for the lack of direction in their lives consumed me.

They reminded me of myself, and so I began to tell my story. At that point, I had their undivided attention.

"My story" began to get off track around the time of the seventh-grade.

I can still remember sitting in Mr. Morgan's seventh-grade social studies class, thinking, "School is stupid! I do not want to be here, but I do want to be around the girls at school and the fun times with my buddies."

I made up my mind right then that I was only going to do just enough to get by in school and enjoy myself. I was willing to do almost anything for a laugh. As I got into high school, this would lead to more undesirable results like drinking, doing drugs, and getting in trouble with the law.

Despite all of that, my ninth-grade English teacher, Mrs. Shirley Albritton, saw something in me and attempted to engage and encourage me. She once told me that I wrote and communicated well.

That wasn't cool or entertaining to anyone, so I just ignored her. I certainly didn't want any of my friends to hear her say that about me.

I did manage to graduate from high school with a low "C" average. Other than barely graduating, the only thing I accomplished was achieving the distinction of being voted "Class Clown" of my senior class. There are no scholarships or trophies awarded with that distinguished honor!

I will never forget graduation night. While most of my fellow students were excited, I was afraid. I wanted to stay in school so that I could continue having a good time. All my friends were looking forward to starting careers, entering the military, or going to college. I had not prepared or planned for anything after graduation. The empty future in front of me was terrifying.

I had several close friends who were planning on attending Florida State University in Tallahassee, Florida in the fall. That was an option, but I was not college material. During my middle school and high school years, when I should have been applying myself to school for the sake of my future, I was living for the now, how I could enjoy it, or make someone else laugh.

I did finally apply to Florida State University only because I thought that maybe it would be a continuation of all the good times that I had in high school. My SAT scores were well below Florida State's minimum score standard to be accepted, but somehow I got in!

Moving to a larger college town like Tallahassee, Florida, from a small town like Live Oak presented its own challenges. Especially with the alcohol, drugs, and all-night partying that was available.

During my first quarter at Florida State, I made three Fs and a D. The second quarter, I made three Fs and an F. Needless to say, it was not long before I received a letter from the dean's office telling me that I was expelled. At about the same time, I had my driver's license suspended for multiple tickets and arrests.

There I was at the age of twenty, kicked out of school, no driver's license, no job, and no future. My father always told me I should be a lawyer because I was a fast talker, and I could convince anyone of anything. He should know, for during my teenage years, he spent a lot of time with me before several county judges. He would always say, "Since you spend so much time at the courthouse, you should consider becoming a lawyer."

Somebody finally shook me up one day when they said, "If you don't get a plan for your life, you're going to end up in prison or worse, dead!"

The truth was I had friends that were in prison and others who had died. That hit a little too close to home.

It was time! I was ready to do something with my life. I committed myself to get back into school, leaving the alcohol and drugs alone and abandoning the aimless way I was living. I was ready to come up with a plan for my life.

I discovered that drugs, alcohol, premarital sex, gangs, violence, bullying, and failing grades are not the real problems. They are symptoms of a much bigger problem; not having a plan, dream, or vision for one's life. I realized that if you don't know where you're going, you'll take every road.

That was me. I was taking every dead-end road because I did not have a destination. Of six kids in my family at that time, not one of us had yet received a college degree. So that was my plan. I enrolled at Tallahassee Community College and received an associate's degree. I then re-enrolled at Florida State University and earned a bachelor's degree in criminology. In 1983, I was the first one in my family to graduate from college.

The next fall, my sister and I moved to Oklahoma to attend Rhema Bible Training Center for two years. After graduating from Rhema, I came back to Live Oak in 1985 to start my Christian ministry career.

After telling my story that day in Berrien County High School, I walked off the stage, and Cyndi (Hayes) Skierski, a young lady in our youth ministry who was helping us with FutureNow, exclaimed, "What you just did was incredible!"

That day, God gave me a message that was my own. From that day on, every time I speak to a group of students, I share my story, much like Joseph Jennings shared his story back in 1990 at my first school assembly.

I tell students that what you have experienced today – the music, dramas, videos, and stories – are all about determining your talents and skills, developing a plan based on them, and pursuing those dreams.

The education system helps you determine your own particular skill sets or talents and then helps you develop them to the best of your ability. If there is no application on your part in school, you will never discover your gifts and talents, and you will hate the life you are left with when you leave this all behind. The gift that I did not even know I had brought me here today, and there is greatness in all of you!

Do you remember that ninth-grade English teacher who tried to help me locate my gifts and abilities, Mrs. Shirley Albritton? One day I ran into her at the grocery store, and I apologized for not allowing her to do her job and help me find and develop my gifts.

I went on to ask students if perhaps many of them are just drifting through school, doing time like I was. Not allowing the education system to help them plan and prepare for their future because they have not been applying themselves or availing themselves of what was being offered.

I strongly suggest that they find a teacher, coach, or administrator and write them a note or apologize to them face-to-face for their behavior. I told them, "Begin today to turn your life around."

When I say this to students, I often have them give a round of applause to the faculty and administration, first for all they do on a daily basis, and secondly to thank them for allowing them to have this assembly program with

FutureNow. One of the last things that I tell students is:

> "Don't make the same mistake I made by not taking your future seriously. You cannot be anything you want to be. That is a lie! But you can be what you are gifted to be. Remember, your future starts now!"

CHAPTER NINE

# The Night Event: A Time of Decision

At the end of the FutureNow assembly program, we have a student Christian club member announce that the local chapter of their club has invited us back that night as their guest for a special event. The student club members then distribute night event fliers to the students as they are leaving the assembly.

Weeks before the day of the assembly, we meet with local churches in the area to garner support and take part in the outreach. Some of the students may already know about the nighttime outreach event via their churches because of this community support. But still, many students in the schools are unaware of the event that is to follow that night.

We have discovered during our eighteen years of holding these events that the more the community churches and the local Christian students promote the night event, the more unchurched students will attend.

Active Christian community involvement increases the likelihood of "herd mentality" taking place. Herd mentality is a term that describes how groups of people are influenced by their peers to adopt certain behaviors on a mostly emotional, rather than rational basis.

I grew up on a farm, and I saw firsthand how this works. If a group of cows in a herd starts running in one particular direction, all the other cows in the herd will follow.

If the churched students are talking up and excited about the event, more of the unchurched students will attend the night event.

This also works in the negative. In communities where the church-attending students do not take part, the unchurched students stay away in droves.

When we first started holding the night events, we would open up in prayer, followed by a time of worship. That format caused many people to get up and leave as soon as they realized it was a Christian program. A pastor once asked me a thought-provoking question after attending one of our night events, "Are you trying to have a church service or an evangelistic outreach?"

I wasn't sure how to answer that question. He suggested that I not open in prayer or play worship music if I was trying to do an evangelistic outreach.

We made those changes to our night program and now begin the events with positive, upbeat non-church music. We then transition into humorous, more entertaining dramas that make people laugh.

At the end of a video testimony, we present a message declaring Jesus as the One who gives us our gifts, talents, and visions. It is Jesus who helps people get off drugs, clean up their lives, and promises an everlasting future and hope.

After the last drama/video, I walk out and introduce myself as founder and director of FutureNow.

I remind them of "my story" that I shared during the daytime assembly at school and how I received a vision for my life to go back to school and graduate with a college degree.

But this time, I add that on the same day I decided to go back to college and get my degree, I made a much greater decision. My brother Steve had left behind a book in my apartment entitled *Words* by Kenneth Hagin.

I wasn't much of a reader at the time, so it was a good thing the book was small. I picked it up and read it. In the back of the book, it had a prayer to pray to receive Jesus Christ as Lord and Savior.

Then I share with the crowd, "I prayed that prayer and this same Jesus became the Lord of my life, and that is the real reason why I am here talking to you tonight."

I tell them that even our name FutureNow comes from Jeremiah 29:11.

> "For I know the plans I have for you," declares the LORD, "plans to prosper

> you and not to harm you, plans to give
> you hope and a future." (Jeremiah 29:11
> NIV)

"There are spiritual gifts and future plans that God has for each and every one of you," I explain. "But they do not start functioning until you connect with the One that gives those gifts and has those plans! He wants a relationship with each one of you so that you can receive those gifts and future that He has planned for you."

The scriptures I prayed to receive Jesus Christ as Lord are found in Romans:

> "That if you confess with your mouth the
> Lord Jesus and believe in your heart that
> God raised  Him from the dead, you
> will be saved. For with the heart, one
> believes unto righteousness, and with the
> mouth, confession is made unto
> salvation." (Romans 10:9-10)

Finally, I ask the question, "If you died tonight, do you know for sure that Jesus is your Lord, and that you are a born-again child of God?"

I tell them that I have asked that question to thousands of students hundreds of times. Over the years, some of the answers I hear are, "I think so," or "I hope so."

That would be like me saying, "I think I am a man" or "I hope I am a man." You should know you are a Christian as much as you know you are male or female.

> These things I have written to you who believe in the name of the Son of God, *that you may know that you have eternal life*. (I John 5:13a)

> We *know* that we have passed from death to life, because we love the brethren. He who does not love his brother abides in death. (I John 3:14)

Students many times answer that question with, "Well, I love God!" The problem with that answer is that "love" is an over-used word in our culture. We throw it around with little or no real meaning.

People say they love peanut butter or they love hunting and fishing. People say they love their job, but continue to show up late to work every day. Or they say they love their spouse, but they cheat on them.

Real love, the God-kind of love, is a commitment.

> If anyone *loves* Me, he will keep My word; and My Father will love him, and We will come to him and make Our home with him. (John 14:23)

Love is following Jesus and not looking back. It's saying, "I have decided to follow Jesus. Though none go with me, still I will follow."

I instruct the crowd, "Based on everything you have seen and heard tonight, you have a decision to make. If you want Jesus Christ to be the Lord of your life or you want to recommit your life to Him, when I count to three, I want you to shoot your hand in the air. I am not asking you to bow your head or close your eyes. I want you to look me in the eye and boldly shoot your hand in the air and keep it there if you have decided to make Jesus the Lord of your life. If tomorrow a terrorist group was invading this community, and I asked for a show of hands of who would join me in the morning to defend our community, I would not ask you to bow your heads and to quickly slip your hand up and hurriedly put it back down. No, I would want you to look me in the eyes and boldly declare you would be there with me in the morning."

I continue, "The decision that I am asking you to make right now is even more crucial than you showing up to defend your community. This is life or death! This decision is your life, and it is for eternity. I am asking for every head up and every eye open. Do you want to make Jesus Christ the Lord of your life, or to recommit your life to Him? Not think so, or hope so, but know so! When I count to three, I want you to shoot your hand in the air."

It never fails that when I count to three, hands are going up all over the room. Boys, girls, men, women, young, and old alike respond to the invitation.

For those with their hands in the air, I ask them to please stand to their feet, and as the band begins to play, to meet me in front of the stage. I would not trade anything for the joy and the presence of God that fills that auditorium and our hearts when I see the faces of those people coming willingly to give their lives to God!

Numerous times I am overcome with emotion. I thought it was just me, but many times I see band members weeping as people are coming forward to pray.

Once, we had a guitarist unstrap his guitar and prostrate himself right there on stage before the Lord. That stage becomes their altar and literally transforms into a Holy Place.

The hard work of coordinating the assembly dates, the countless logistical meetings of getting the community churches involved, the late-night load-ins, the build-up of the stage, the set-up of the sound and video equipment, and late-night teardowns, are all worth it for that one moment!

Before we pray, I instruct those responding, "This is the same prayer that I prayed when I made Jesus Christ the Lord of my life back in 1981."

I tell them, "Now, I want you to bow your head and close your eyes. Pray this prayer with me and mean it from your heart … 'Father God, I come to you in the name of Jesus. God, you said in your Word, in Romans 10:9-10, that if I confess with my mouth Jesus as my Lord and believe in my heart that You, God, raised Him from the dead, I would be saved. For with my heart, I believe, and with my mouth, confession is made to eternal life. Thank you, Father, that I am now a child of God! In Jesus' name, Amen!'"

After we pray, the students and parents down front are invited to follow us into the school cafeteria where we have local church volunteers waiting who will help collect their contact information and give them each a Bible.

Before they leave the cafeteria, I always take a few minutes to talk to them about the importance of being involved in a local church. I share with them how I was discipled by two different youth pastors during the early years of my life with Christ. Everything that I learned about youth outreach and evangelism, I learned by being involved in a local church.

Immediately after I got saved in 1981, I started attending Evangel Assembly of God in Tallahassee, Florida while I was going to Florida State University. The youth pastors at Evangel were Steve and Jeri Hill.

Steve, who has since gone home to be with the Lord, had a huge heart for youth outreach and evangelism. He is best known as the lead evangelist of the Brownsville revival in Pensacola, Florida. These meetings drew more than four million people from more than 150 nations to the Brownsville Assembly of God Church.

During this five-year revival, hundreds of thousands wept at the altars, repented of sinful lifestyles and gave their lives to Jesus. Lives were dramatically changed, marriages were restored, and addictions were broken as the gospel of Jesus Christ was presented with clarity.

After the Brownsville revival, Steve Hill and his team continued to hold large arena and stadium crusades around the world. I learned so much about youth ministry from Steve and Jeri Hill.

But during the weekends and summers of my college years, I also was involved in the youth group at my home church of Melody Church in Live Oak, Florida. Phil Underwood was my youth pastor.

The first summer I was saved, he had my sister, Lauren, and I along with several other young people at the church involved in music, drama, and speaking. We spent many weekends traveling to other churches to put on youth events for their youth groups. He would schedule us anywhere he could find a place just to have us involved in ministry of some sort.

Those were crucial formative years and I truly believe they played a huge part in the ministry that I have today. I am still involved in a local church where I continue to grow in the Lord and the knowledge of His Word and am continuing to fulfill the plans that God has for me.

I also share with those who responded to the invitation to not let the devil, friends, or even family talk them out of their decision to make Jesus the Lord of their life.

"When the devil puts thoughts in your head that make you question whether you are saved," I explain, "Go back to Romans 10:9-10, which are the scriptures that you prayed and acted upon tonight."

The last thing we discuss with them before they are released to go back to the gym and rejoin their family and friends is that as exciting as this was, what is more exciting is the real revival that can begin tomorrow.

I ask the question, "How many of you know someone who couldn't come back tonight for some reason or another? When you go back to school or work tomorrow, you begin to share with others what happened to you tonight, and you can pray that same prayer in Romans 10:9-10 with them. They, too, can receive Jesus Christ as Lord. That's when the real revival will break out."

CHAPTER TEN

# Where We Are Now

At this writing, I am entering my 35th year in full-time youth ministry, seventeen years as a youth pastor, and eighteen years with FutureNow.

Many years ago, a great friend and mentor, Pastor Bernie McLaughlin from Kilwinning, Scotland, told me that God would never take me out of my area of influence.

My area of influence is undoubtedly public schools. I believe that it is easier to take the message of Christ to them than to try and get them to come to us.

After all, the great commission says, "Go into all the world and preach the gospel," not "invite them to come to see you."

Pastor L. A. Joiner, who has been a spiritual mentor to me as well, told me the Lord gave him Acts 1:8 to share with me.

> And you shall be witnesses to Me in Jerusalem, and all Judea and Samaria, and to the end of the earth. (Acts 1:8b)

The Lord showed me that Jerusalem was in reference to my geographical area of influence, and from that point, my influence would spread to other geographic areas.

Originally, the hope of FutureNow was to be able to go into every middle school and high school in America. After a few years, I realized that would be humanly impossible. According to the Department of Education, National Center for Education Statistics (2016), there were over 70,000 public and private secondary schools (middle schools and high schools) in the United States.

At the rate of one school per day, it would take 100 years to visit all those schools. How could we reach all those kids?

To further emphasize the urgent need of our type of ministry, a 2004 Barna Research report stated that, "For years, church leaders have heard the claims that ninety percent of Christians accept Jesus before age eighteen."

In other words, there is only a ten percent chance someone will become a Christian after they graduate from high school. A more recent Barna study shows that "nearly half of all Americans who accept Jesus Christ as their Savior do so before reaching the age of thirteen."

This new data indicates that there is only a fifty percent chance someone will become a Christian after their thirteenth birthday.

If we believe this is true, we should be running to the schools. We have so much work to do, and I am constantly reminded of how little time we have left to make a lasting impact for Christ in the youth of America by that word of prophecy that was handed to me on a corner of a church bulletin so many years ago which said, "The longer you wait, the less people you will reach."

This drove me to my knees.

I recently heard Josh McDowell, evangelist, speaker, and author, say ninety-seven percent of thirteen- to seventeen-year-olds are currently using at least one of the seven major online platforms. Josh said there is only a ten percent chance someone will become a Christian by age twelve, because of this social media revolution.

In 2011, the social media frenzy took off as Facebook became the largest online photo host. In the fall of that year, we decided FutureNow needed an online presence to connect with and reach middle and high school students.

We set a date of February 1st, 2012 to kick-off a video program on Facebook entitled "Daily Stir."

We realized pretty quickly that shooting and editing a video was a lot of work, taking several days to complete. At that rate our "Daily Stir" would be more accurately named the "Monthly Stir." We changed our Daily Stir page from a daily video to a daily written devotional with an occasional video.

Since its inception, I have received responses to the Daily Stir from all over the world. I recently received this comment from Malawi, Africa:

> "May the God of our Lord Jesus Christ increase your understanding in His word. We are really blessed with your posts and also we are taking your messages as our daily teachings in our gatherings and our services. We are not the same as we used to be. Man of God, we are your sons and daughters in Christ here in Malawi. God bless you!"

A friend expressed an interest in my Daily Stir posts but didn't want to set up a Facebook account. He asked me if I would email it to him. So, I did. He in turn emailed it to a friend.

About a week or so later he gave me the name of that friend who also wanted to receive the Daily Stir via email. Eventually, I just added my whole contact list to the Daily Stir email list.

It grew so large that it became difficult to maintain in my Outlook account, so I had to enlist the help of two different email services.

One is currently forwarding the Daily Stir to 88 different people and the other forwards it out to over 40 individuals every day.

Today there are over 5,400 subscribers. This large following doesn't include the followers of the Daily Stir who read and share it every day on Facebook or the people who forward the daily emails to their family and friends.

Numerous pastors, youth pastors, Sunday school teachers, and even coaches tell me that they use the Daily Stir as devotionals on a constant basis.

In addition, every person who responds to an invitation to receive Jesus as Lord at our FutureNow events will be subscribed to the Daily Stir.

It is humbling and I am grateful to God and give him all the glory for the impact that the Daily Stir is having in so many lives. (To receive the Daily Stir by email, simply email info@futurenow.us and leave your full name and email address.)

A little over five years ago, I spent a day of fasting and prayer at a friend's cabin in the country. During this time, God told me to draw a circle around Valdosta, Georgia, of about a 100-mile radius. This circle includes a little over forty communities in North Florida and South Georgia. The Lord specifically told me to only go to schools in this area.

I am to be a resource for communities, not a school assembly program that blows in and out of town. We are to be someone the schools can contact as a resource. So, I did just that.

Now, in addition to our school assemblies, we hold Christian club meetings, provide youth services, speak to the schools' sports teams, and take part in area revivals.

Unbelievably, I have even been asked to speak at school faculty meetings. As recently as last year, I was the speaker for an employee luncheon at a county school system. We are invited to schools experiencing tragedies, such as classmates or teachers who have died or families who have lost their homes.

With schools within our 100-mile radius, about an hour and a half drive, we can be there rather quickly. There are not enough guidance counselors to handle all the students who need someone to talk to, so our presence is greatly appreciated.

When a school principal contacts us to come because of some tragedy, we are there – whether it's just to listen, or give support. Whatever the school needs us to do, we will do. We do this in conjunction with local churches, other pastors, youth pastors, and any Christian student-led clubs within the community.

God said that He would help us duplicate this regional outreach ministry.

As I said before, the area around Valdosta (North Florida and South Georgia) is my geographical area of influence per Acts 1:8.

Our 100-mile radius is my Jerusalem. However, eventually and with God's leading, we will be an influence in both our "Judea," "Samaria," and the uttermost parts of the world.

I may not personally go to all those places, but we desire to train other teams to serve in their areas of influence. I believe there are other "Chris Musgroves" out there who are looking and waiting for their "Jerusalems."

We have received calls from all over the United States requesting information for starting FutureNow teams to serve students. We believe it is time to act.

Is God speaking to you about seeing students inspired, motivated, transformed, and then empowered?

We are working tirelessly to fulfill what the Lord has called us to do. We are holding events in more schools and reaching more students. We must inspire young people with vision, purpose, and destiny, culminating in changed lives for the Kingdom of God.

We have a lot of work to do, and we cannot do it without you!

> For, "Everyone who calls on the name of
> the Lord will be saved." How, then, can

> they call on the one they have not believed in? And how can they believe in the one of whom they have not heard? And how can they hear without someone preaching to them? And how can anyone preach *unless they are sent*? As it is written: *"How beautiful are the feet of those who bring good news!"* (Romans 10:13-15 NIV)

Right now, we are renting an office building with an option to buy. We hope to buy the property in the near future as a home base for the ministry.

When we complete that purchase, a generous donor has already offered to provide the materials to build an 8,000 square foot multi-purpose building that we will use as an event and training center.

Everyone has a part to play in reaching these students with the Gospel of Jesus Christ. All FutureNow team members are missionaries to the public schools.

Would you consider partnering with us through your prayers, your involvement as a volunteer, and your financial support. No gift or effort is too small to make a difference.

Are you interested in seeing a FutureNow team started in your area? If so, contact our office for upcoming training dates.

The Future is Now! Be blessed!

> *– Chris Musgrove*
> *Info@futurenow.us*
> *www.chrismusgroveministries.com*
> *Jeremiah 29:11*

# Prayer to Receive Jesus as Lord

Father God,

I come to You in the name of Your Son, Jesus Christ.

You said in Your Word, in Romans 10: 9-10: If I confess with my mouth "Jesus is Lord," and believe in my heart that God raised Him from the dead, I would be saved.

For with my heart I believe, and with my mouth confession is made unto eternal life! So I believe in my heart and I confess with my mouth that Jesus is my Lord! Therefore, I am saved!

Thank you, Lord!

Signed: _____ Date: _____

*We want to help you grow spiritually. It's important to get involved in a local church and read God's Word daily. Use our discipleship program @itsthefollowup (scan the QR code). For questions or help finding a church, contact us at: info@futurenow.us*

ITSTHEFOLLOWUP

For further information about
FutureNow or Chris Musgrove
Ministries, please visit the
ministry websites at:

www.Futurenow.us

www.chrismusgroveministries.com